AF588483

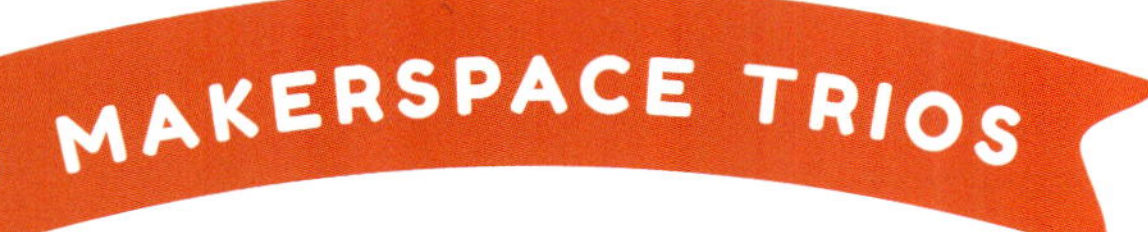

Creating with CHENILLE STEMS, BOTTLES & TISSUE PAPER

Elsie Olson

Consulting Editor, Diane Craig,
M.A./Reading Specialist

Super Sandcastle

An Imprint of Abdo Publishing
abdobooks.com

abdobooks.com

Published by Abdo Publishing, a division of ABDO, PO Box 398166, Minneapolis, Minnesota 55439.

Printed in the United States of America, North Mankato, Minnesota
102021
012022

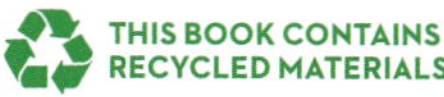

Design: Sarah DeYoung, Mighty Media, Inc.
Production: Mighty Media, Inc.
Editor: Megan Borgert-Spaniol
Cover Photographs: iStockphoto; Mighty Media, Inc.; Shutterstock Images
Interior Photographs: Don Porcella; iStockphoto; Mighty Media, Inc.; PauloMSimoes/Wikimedia Commons; Shutterstock Images; superk8nyc/Flickr

The following manufacturers/names appearing in this book are trademarks: Crayola®, Elmer's®

Library of Congress Control Number: 2021943031

Publisher's Cataloging-in-Publication Data
Names: Olson, Elsie, author.
Title: Creating with chenille stems, bottles & tissue paper / by Elsie Olson
Description: Minneapolis, Minnesota : Abdo Publishing, 2022 | Series: Makerspace trios | Includes online resources and index.
Identifiers: ISBN 9781532196416 (lib. bdg.) | ISBN 9781098218225 (ebook)
Subjects: LCSH: Handicraft--Juvenile literature. | Creative thinking--Juvenile literature. | Pipe cleaner craft--Juvenile literature. | Plastic bottle craft--Juvenile literature. | Paper craft--Juvenile literature. | Mixed media crafts--Juvenile literature.
Classification: DDC 745.5--dc23

Super SandCastle™ books are created by a team of professional educators, reading specialists, and content developers around five essential components—phonemic awareness, phonics, vocabulary, text comprehension, and fluency—to assist young readers as they develop reading skills and strategies and increase their general knowledge. All books are written, reviewed, and leveled for guided reading and early reading intervention programs for use in shared, guided, and independent reading and writing activities to support a balanced approach to literacy instruction.

TO ADULT HELPERS

The projects in this book are fun and simple. There are just a few things to remember to keep kids safe. Some projects may use sharp or hot objects. Also, kids may be using messy supplies. Make sure they protect their clothes and work surfaces. Be ready to offer guidance during brainstorming and assist when necessary.

CONTENTS

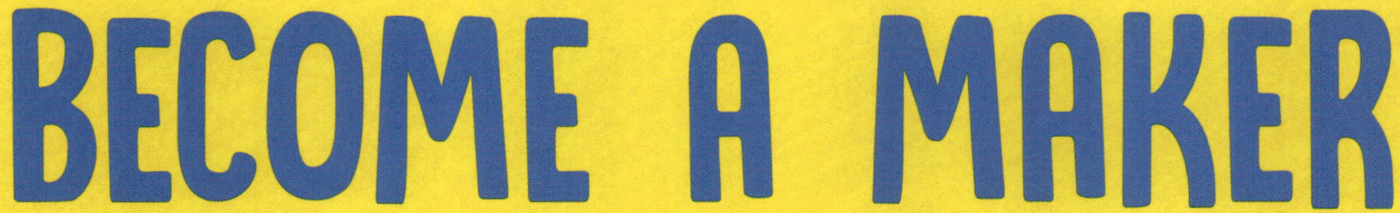

BECOME A MAKER

A makerspace is like a laboratory. It's a place where ideas are formed and problems are solved. Kids like you create amazing things in makerspaces. Many makerspaces are in schools and libraries. But they can also be in kitchens, bedrooms, and backyards. Anywhere can be a makerspace when you use imagination, inspiration, **collaboration**, and problem-solving!

Imagination

This takes you to new places and lets you experience new things. Anything is possible with imagination!

Inspiration

This is the spark that gives you an idea. Inspiration can come from almost anywhere!

Makerspace Toolbox

Collaboration

Makers work together. They ask questions and get ideas from everyone around them. Collaboration solves problems that seem impossible.

Problem-Solving

Things often don't go as planned when you're creating. But that's part of the fun! Find creative solutions to any problem that comes up. These will make your project even better.

EXPLORE CHENILLE STEMS

Chenille stems are twisted wires covered in soft fibers. They are often used for cleaning narrow spaces, such as tubes. They can be used as twist ties to secure bags or cords. Chenille stems are also a popular crafting material!

Chenille Stem Properties

- Colorful
- Flexible
- Long
- Soft

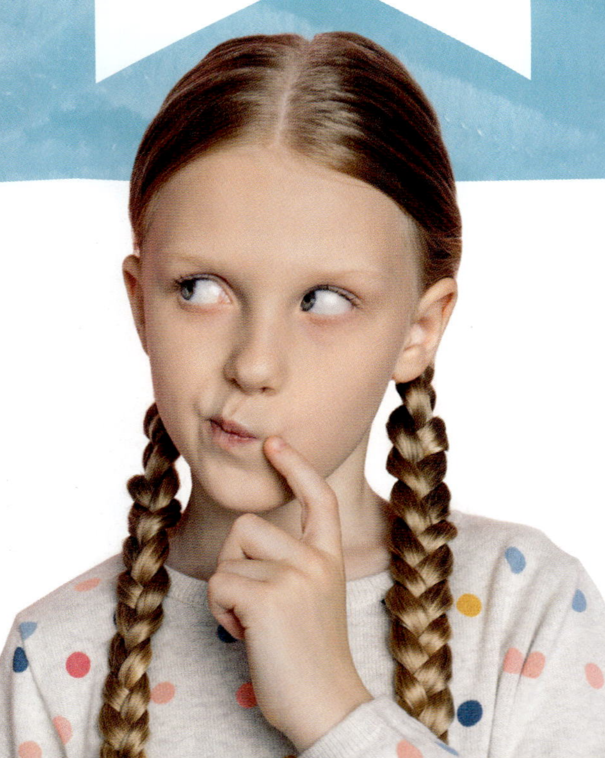

How Can You Use Chenille Stems?

Chenille stems have many standard uses. But they can be used however you like in a makerspace! Let your imagination wander. What would it look like to use chenille stems in a new way?

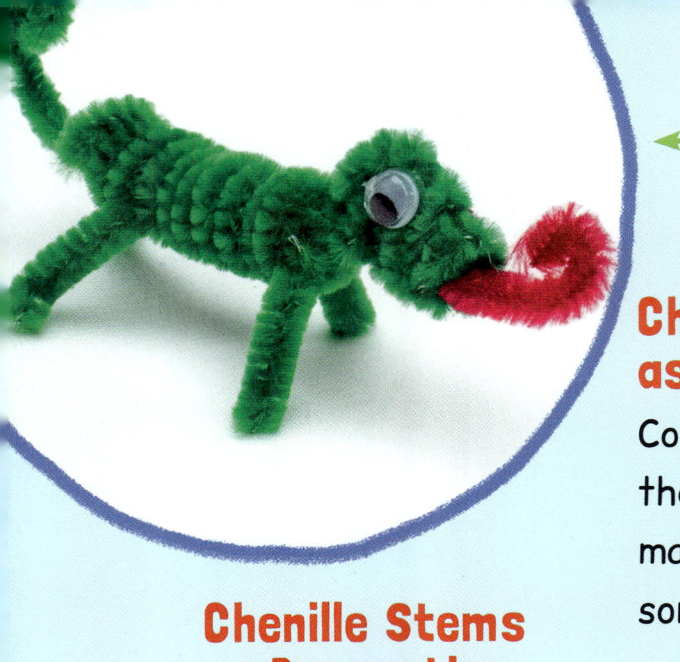

Chenille Stems as a Base

Could you twist them together to make an animal or some other shape?

Chenille Stems Converted

Could you strip the fibers off a chenille stem to leave the wire?

Chenille Stems as Decoration

Could you make flames or other cool details with them?

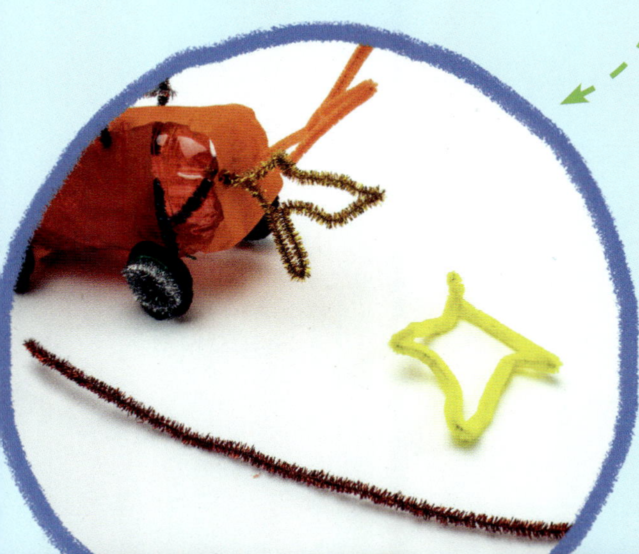

Chenille Stems as a Tool

Could you use them to secure two materials together or hang a project?

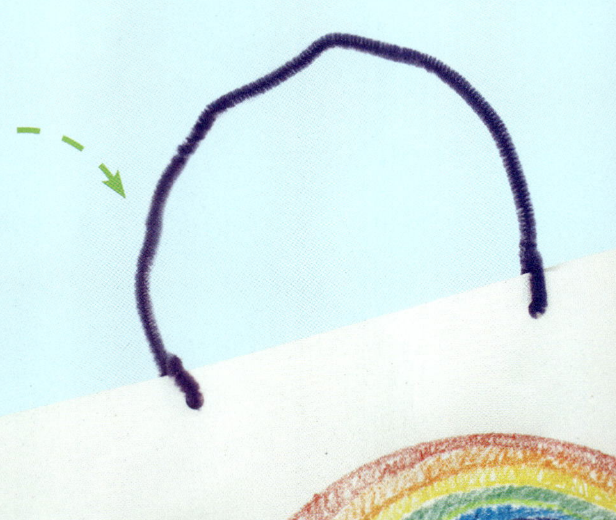

EXPLORE BOTTLES

You probably come across bottles almost every day. These narrow **containers** are used to hold water, juice, and other drinks. Many bottles are made of plastic or glass. Most have a cap made of plastic or metal. Some bottles are **designed** to be used again and again!

Bottle Properties

- Hollow
- Narrow neck
- See-through
- Sturdy

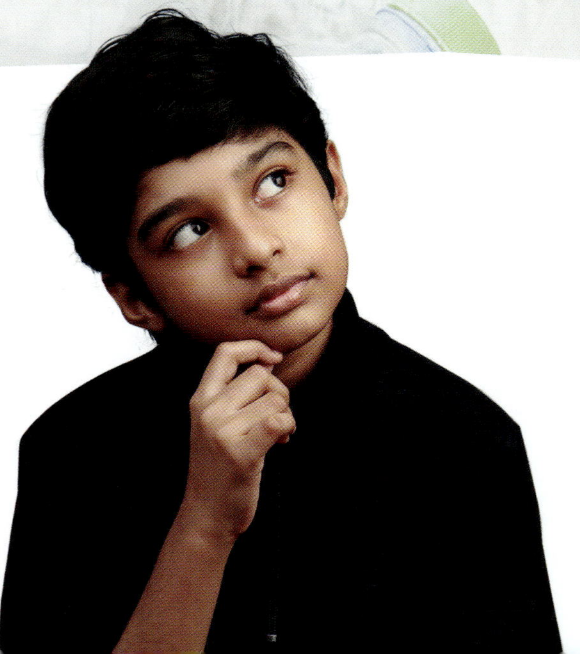

How Can You Use Bottles?

Bottles are most often used to carry liquids. But they can be used however you like in a makerspace! Let your imagination wander. What would it look like to use bottles in a new way?

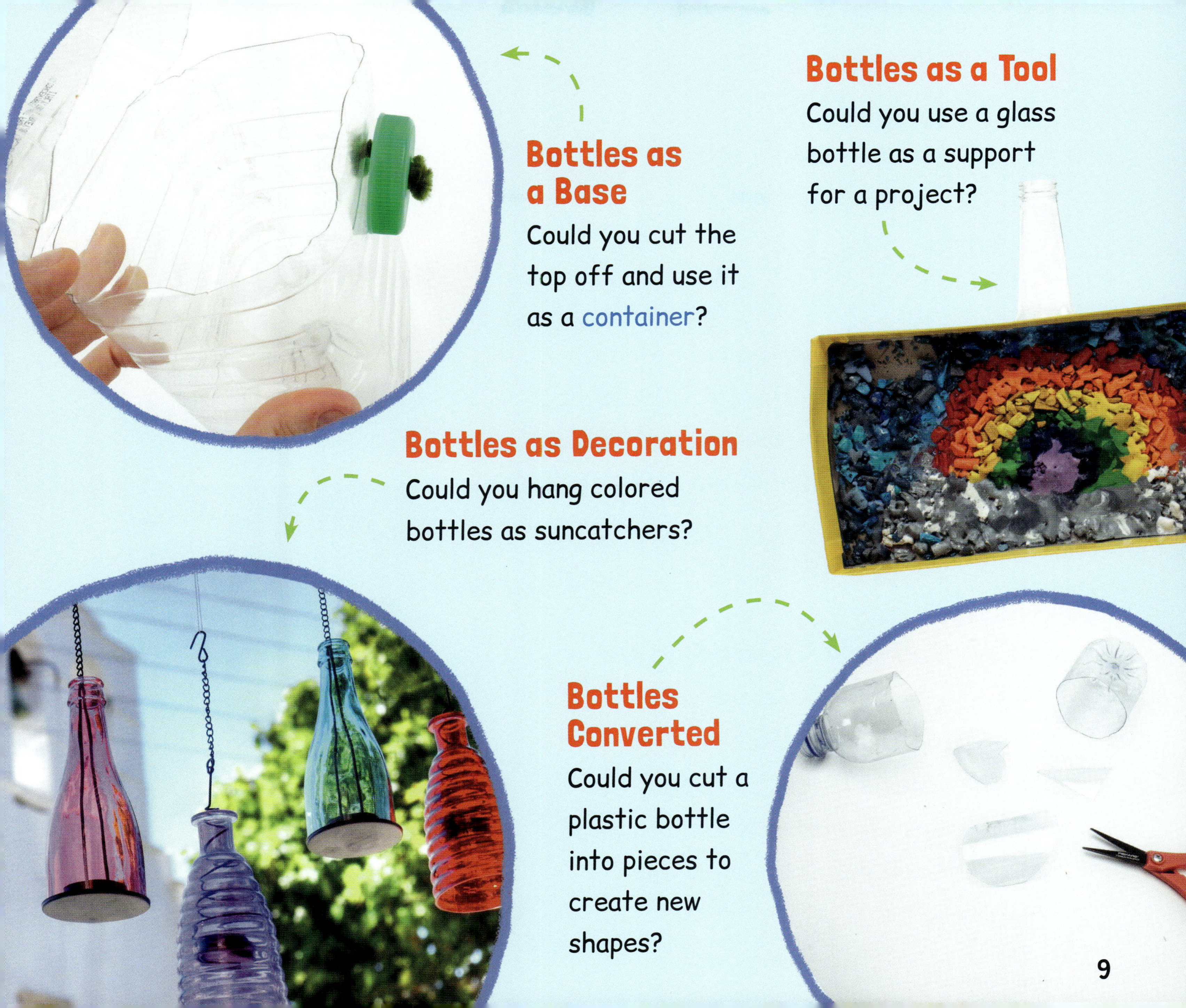

Bottles as a Tool

Could you use a glass bottle as a support for a project?

Bottles as a Base

Could you cut the top off and use it as a container?

Bottles as Decoration

Could you hang colored bottles as suncatchers?

Bottles Converted

Could you cut a plastic bottle into pieces to create new shapes?

EXPLORE TISSUE PAPER

Have you ever opened a gift bag filled with tissue paper? This paper-based product is often used to wrap gifts or fill gift bags. People also wrap breakable items in tissue paper to protect them.

Tissue Paper Properties

- Colorful
- Cuttable
- Soft
- Thin

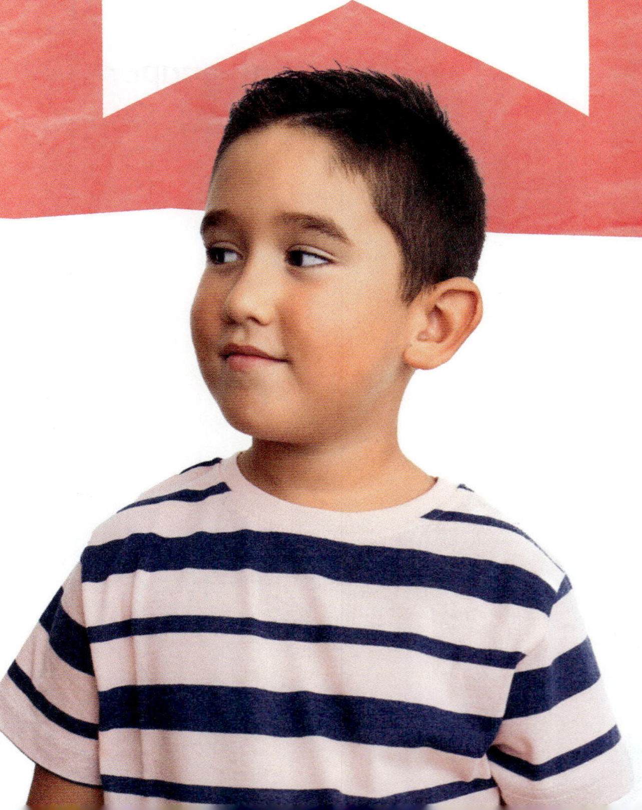

How Can You Use Tissue Paper?

Tissue paper is often used for gift wrapping. But it can be used however you like in a makerspace! Let your imagination wander. What would it look like to use tissue paper in a new way?

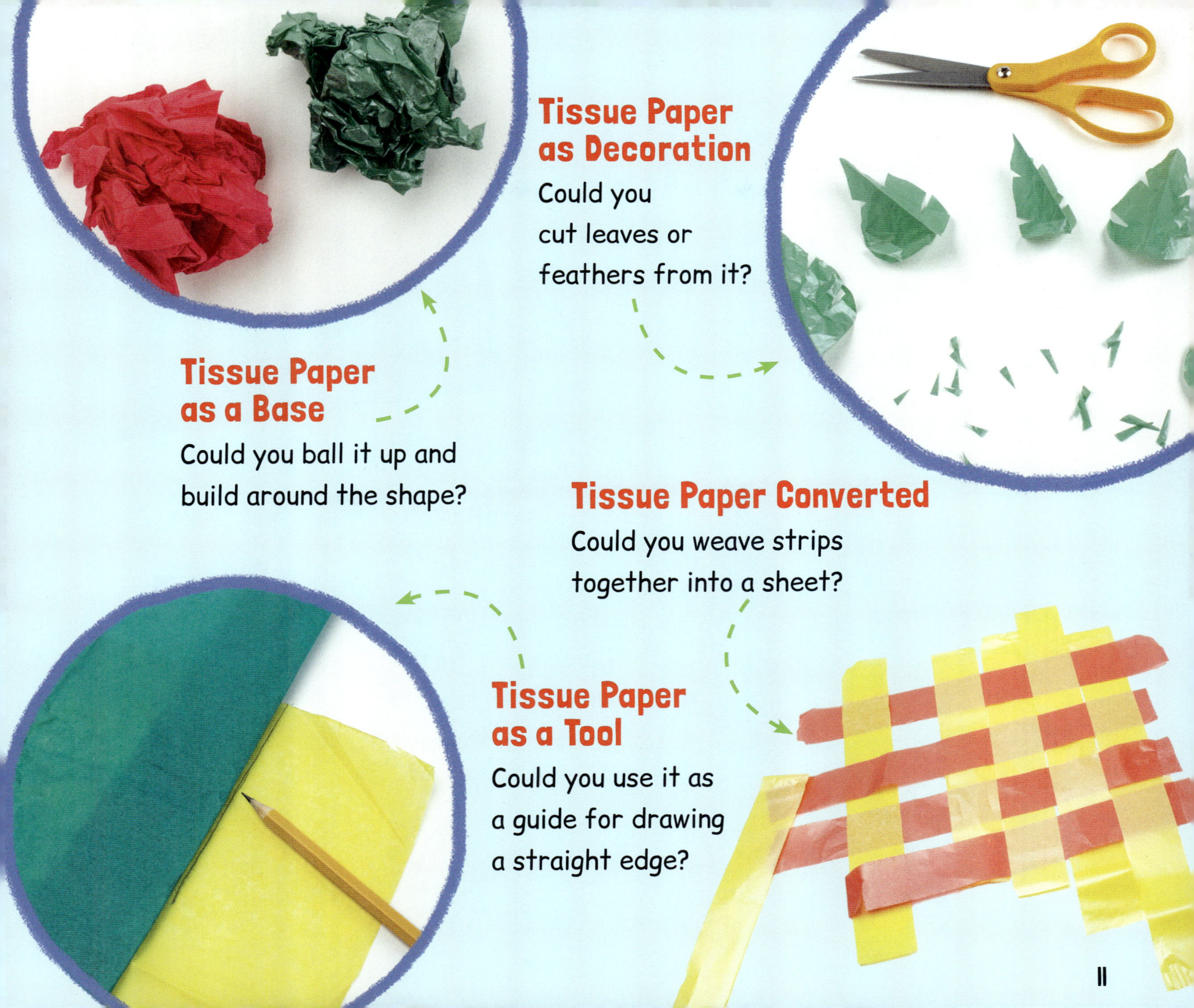

Tissue Paper as Decoration

Could you cut leaves or feathers from it?

Tissue Paper as a Base

Could you ball it up and build around the shape?

Tissue Paper Converted

Could you weave strips together into a sheet?

Tissue Paper as a Tool

Could you use it as a guide for drawing a straight edge?

GET INSPIRED

People have used chenille stems, bottles, and tissue paper in all kinds of creative ways. Let these examples spark your imagination!

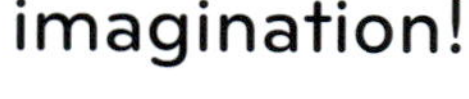

Don Porcella is an artist known for making fun sculptures out of chenille stems.

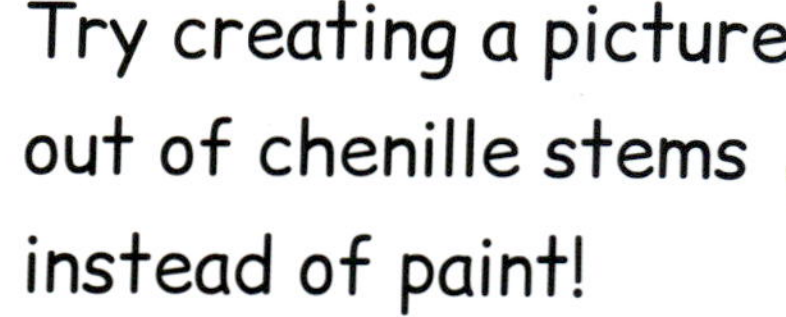

Try creating a picture out of chenille stems instead of paint!

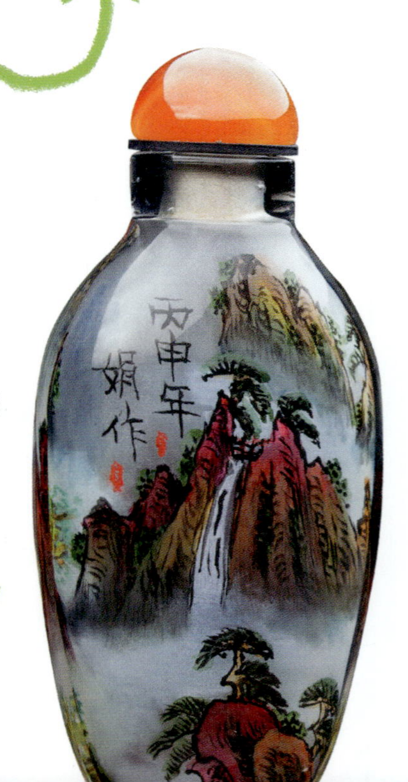

Inner painting is a Chinese art form in which artists paint scenes on the insides of glass bottles.

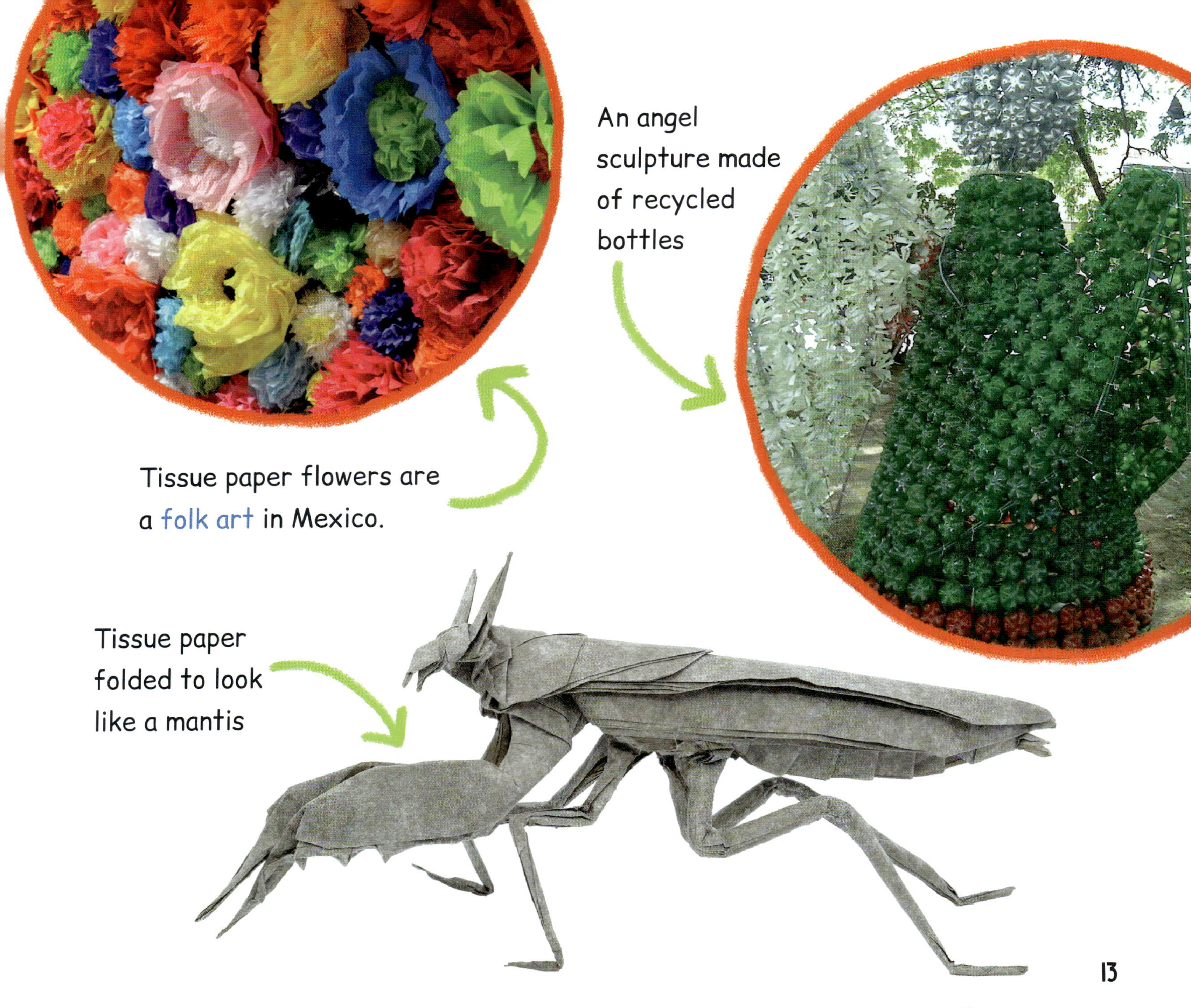

An angel sculpture made of recycled bottles

Tissue paper flowers are a folk art in Mexico.

Tissue paper folded to look like a mantis

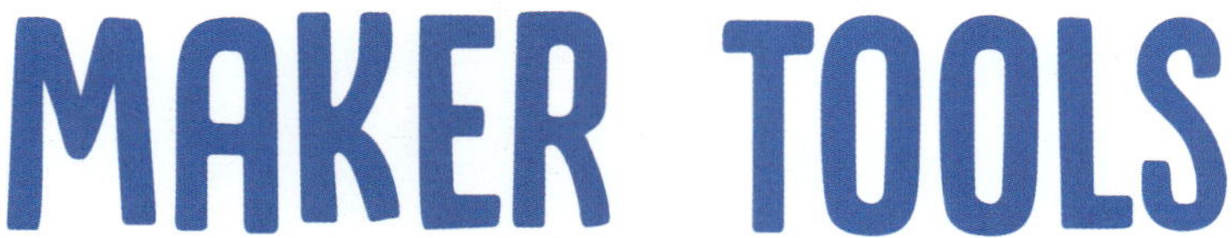

MAKER TOOLS

Are you inspired? Have you brainstormed some makerspace projects? It's time to gather your chenille stems, bottles, and tissue paper. You may also need a few everyday tools to cut and connect your primary materials.

wire cutter

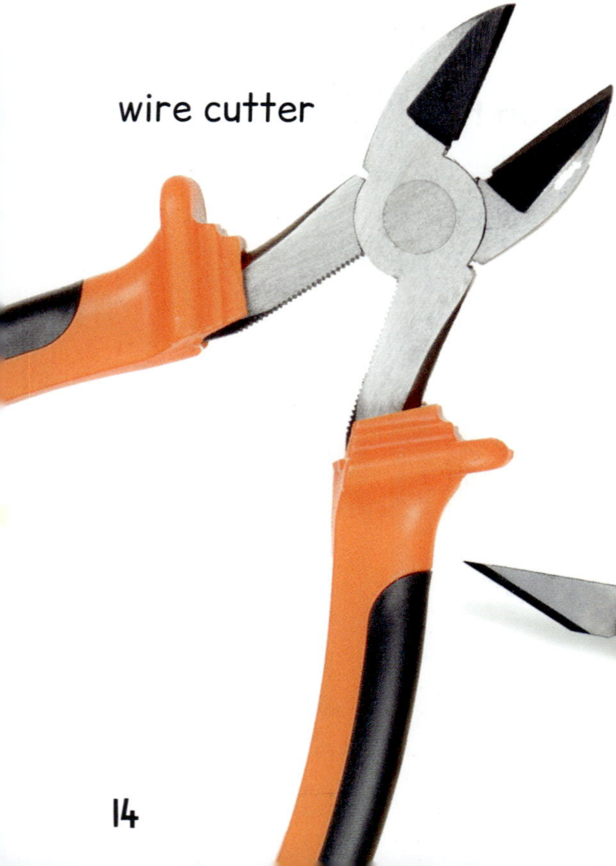

scissors

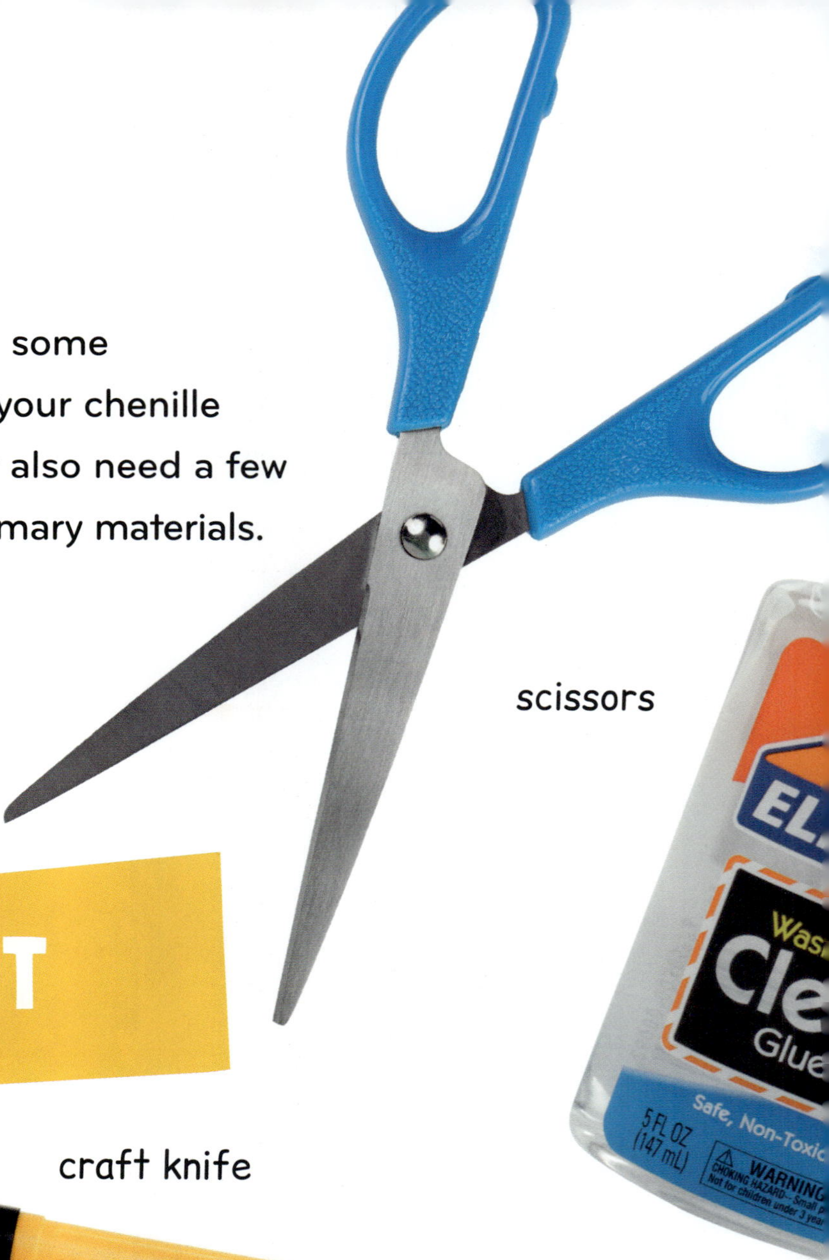

CUT

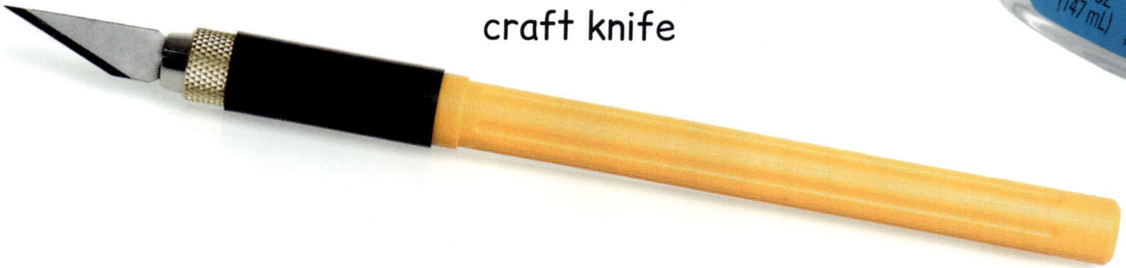

craft knife

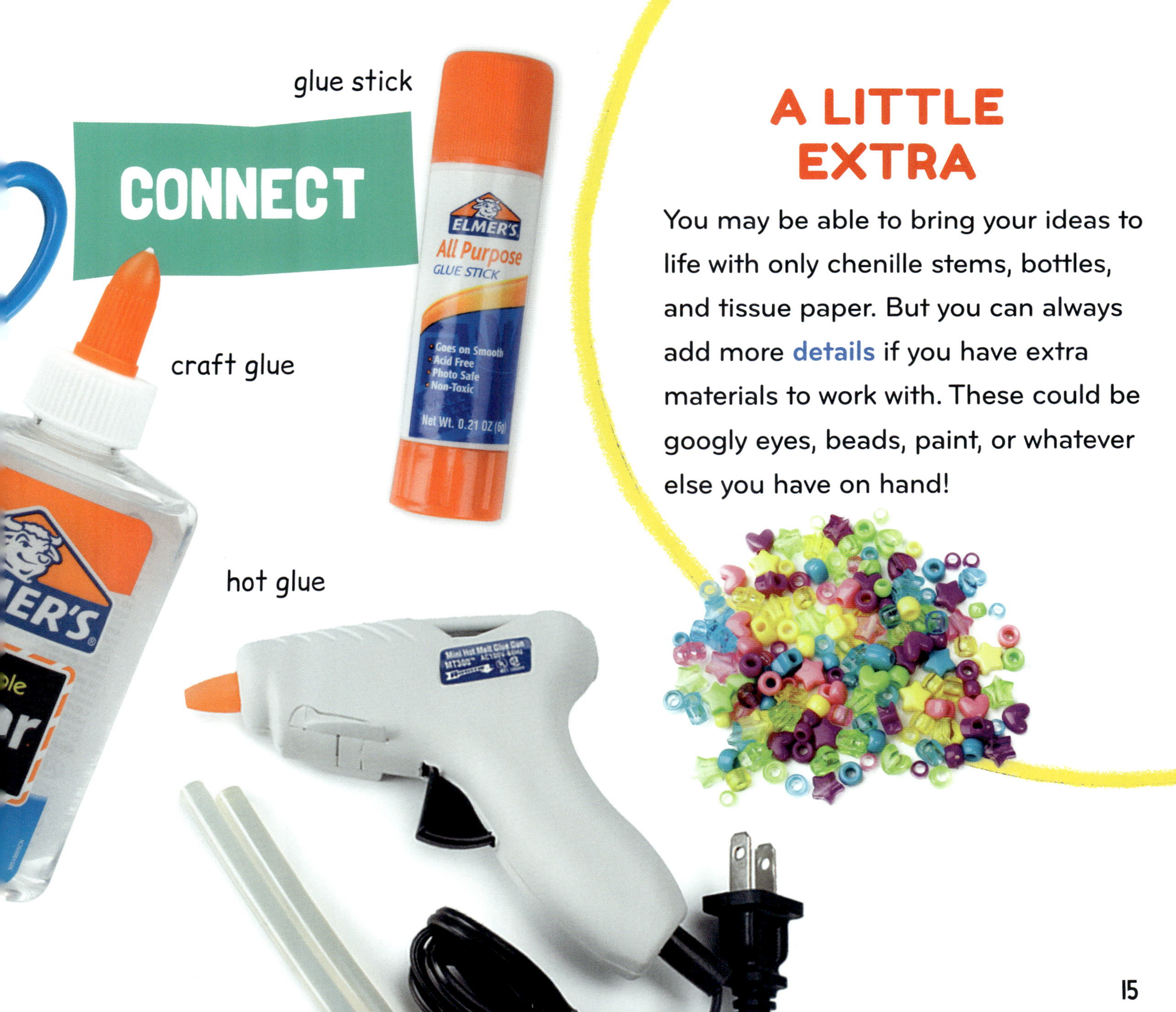

A LITTLE EXTRA

You may be able to bring your ideas to life with only chenille stems, bottles, and tissue paper. But you can always add more **details** if you have extra materials to work with. These could be googly eyes, beads, paint, or whatever else you have on hand!

MAKING YOUR MAKERSPACE

You can let your imagination run wild in a makerspace. But be sure to follow these rules to stay safe and be respectful.

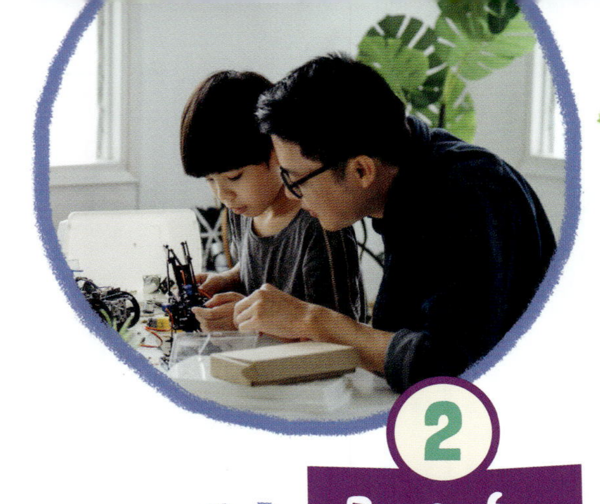

2 Be safe

Ask an adult for help when using sharp or hot tools, such as craft knives or glue guns.

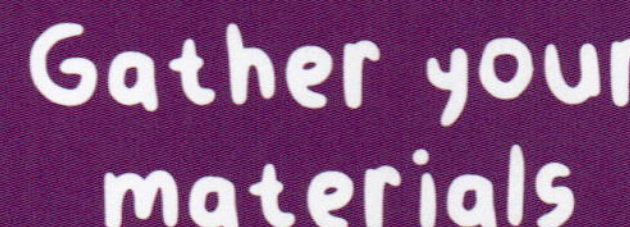

1 Gather your materials

Make sure an adult says it's OK to use what you gather.

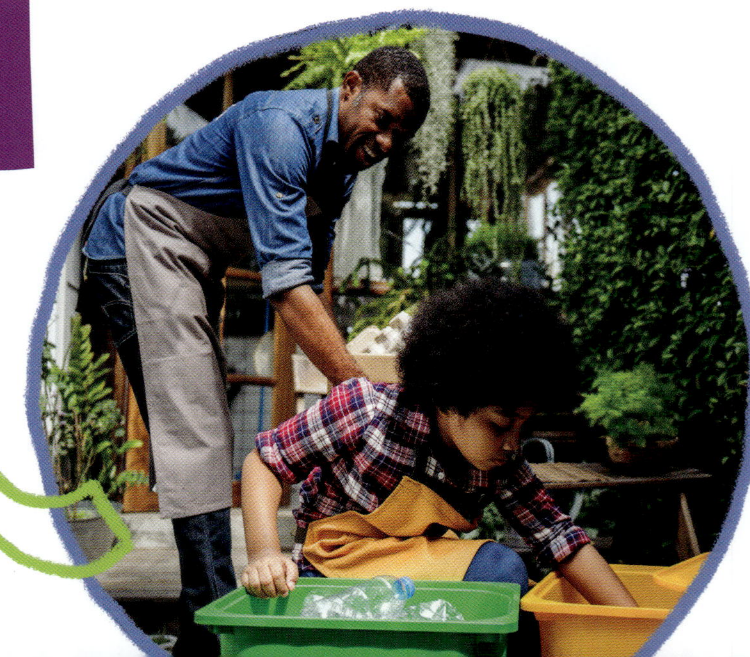

Share the space

Share supplies and space with other makers. You can invite them to share their ideas if you're feeling stuck!

Keep trying

Don't give up when things don't go exactly as planned. Instead, think about the problem you are having. What are some ways to solve it?

Clean up

Put away materials. Find a safe space to store unfinished projects until next time. And clean up any scraps, spills, or messes you made.

DISPLAY IT

Create an artwork from chenille stems, bottles, and tissue paper. Then put it on display!

Glue tissue paper and chenille stems to bottle caps to make little bugs.

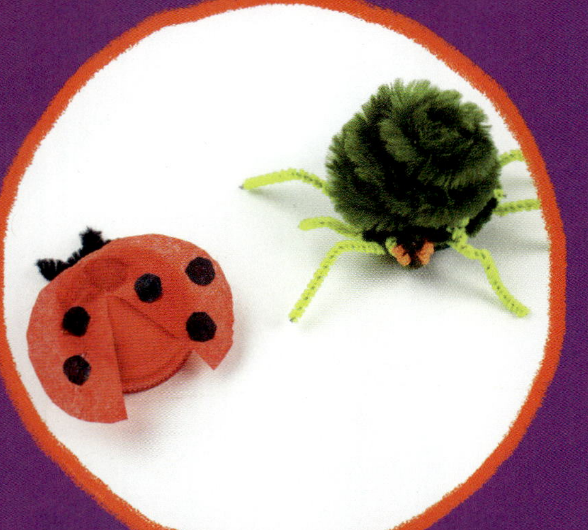

Wrap chenille stems around a pencil to make coiled stems.

Twist chenille stems around folded pieces of tissue paper to make flowers.

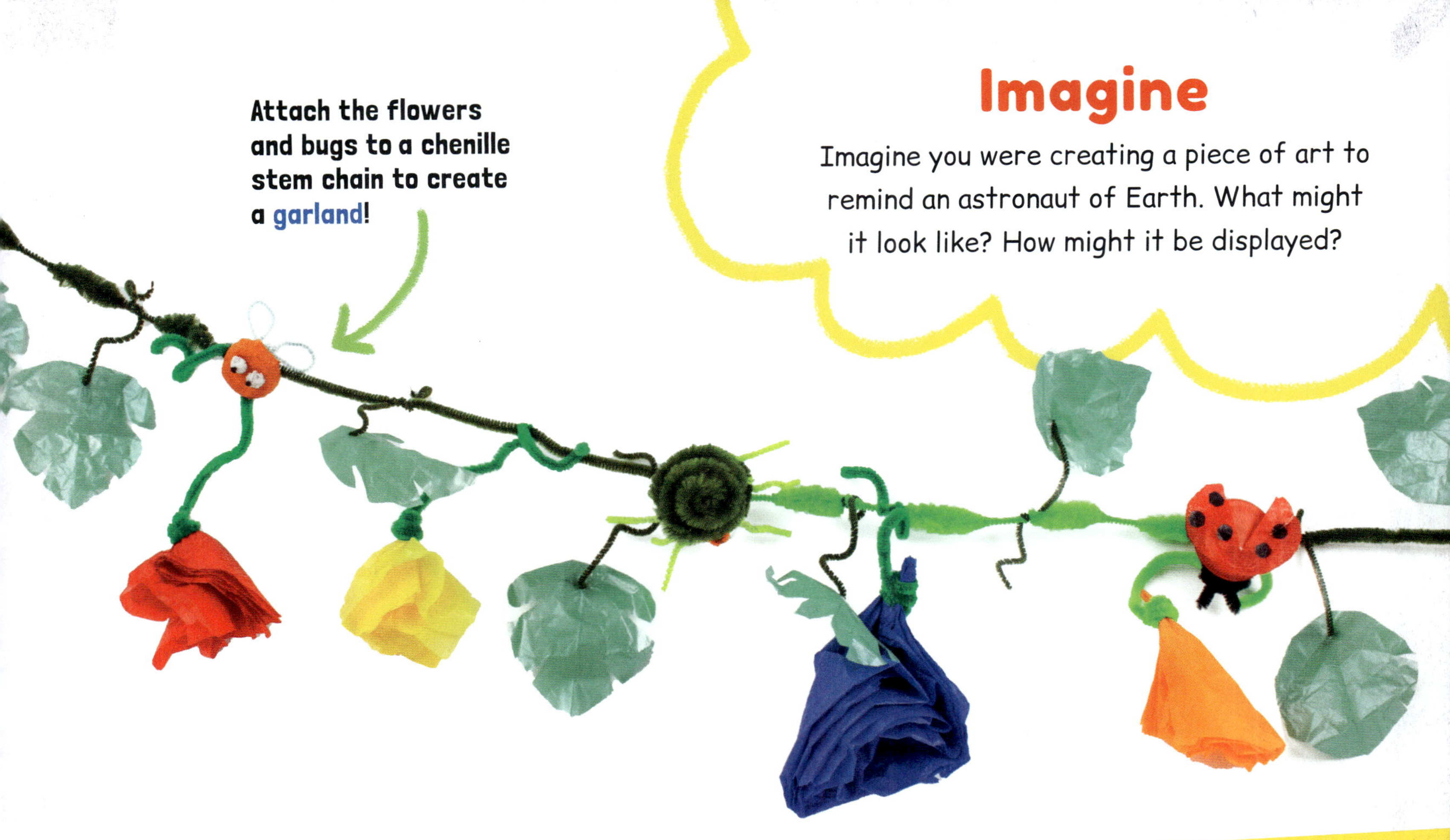

Imagine

Imagine you were creating a piece of art to remind an astronaut of Earth. What might it look like? How might it be displayed?

Your Turn!

Could you cut up chenille stems to make a mosaic?

What artwork could you create from a soda bottle or shampoo bottle?

Could you create a 3D painting using rolled-up tissue paper?

WEAR IT

What wearable clothing or accessories could you make from chenille stems, bottles, and tissue paper?

Cut a flap in an empty bottle to make a pouch.

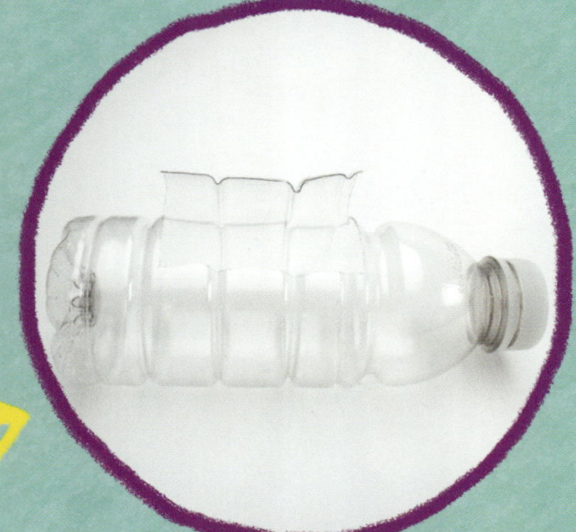

Braid together chenille stems and twisted tissue paper to make a belt.

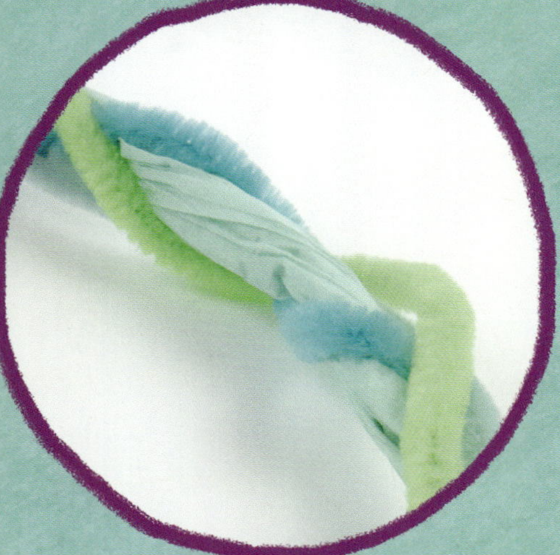

Poke a hole in the bottom of the bottle and the bottle cap. Push the ends of your belt through the holes.

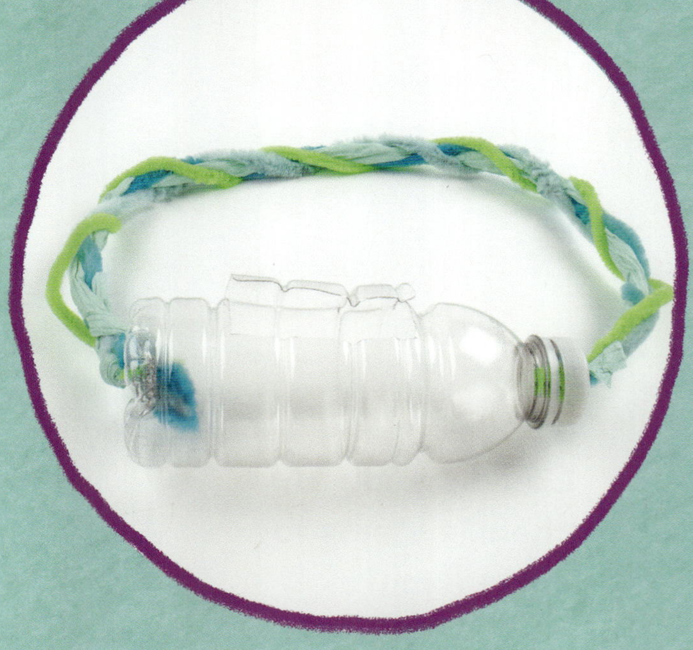

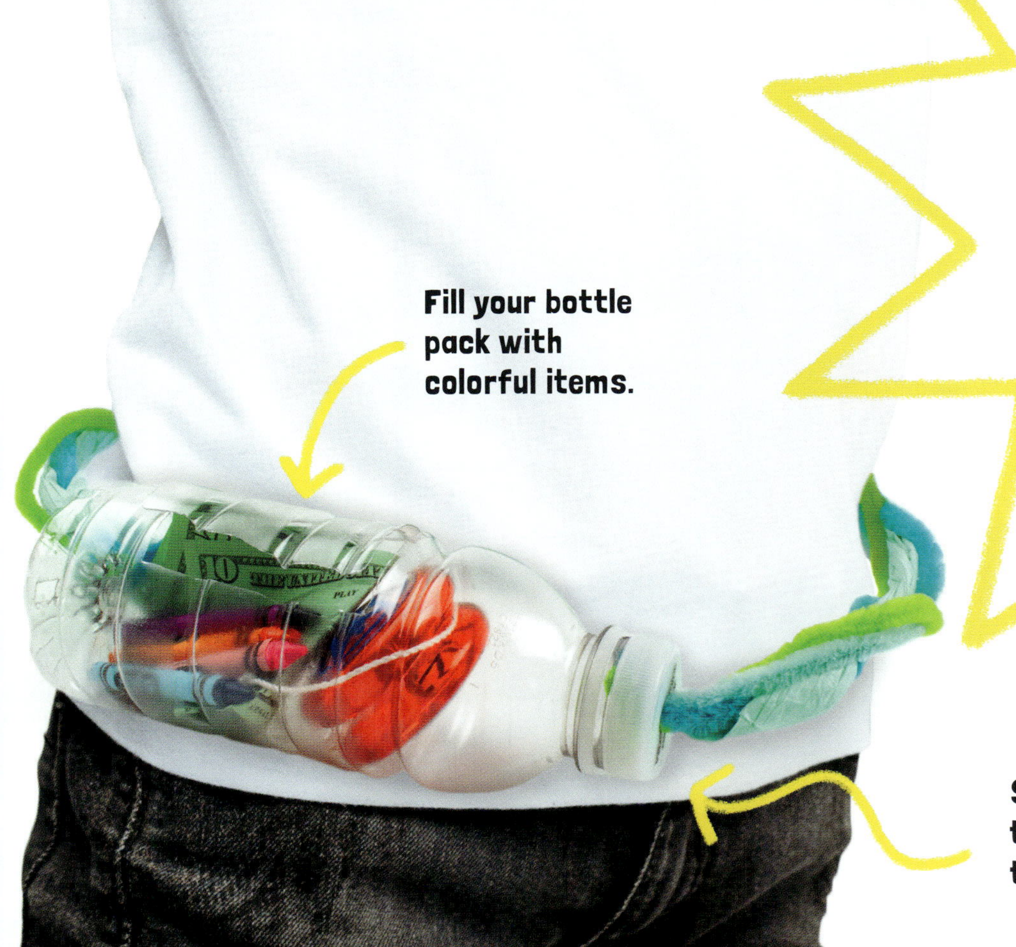

Fill your bottle pack with colorful items.

Screw and unscrew the cap to put on and take off your pack.

Problem-Solve

Every problem has more than one solution. Is your bottle pack too small? You could add a second bottle. Or you could use chenille stems to hang objects off it!

Your Turn!

How could you make a key chain out of chenille stems?

Could you cut rings out of a plastic bottle to make bracelets?

Could you twist and braid tissue paper into a headband?

USE IT

Think of an item you need. Then **design** it! Chenille stems, bottles, and tissue paper provide many options for functional projects.

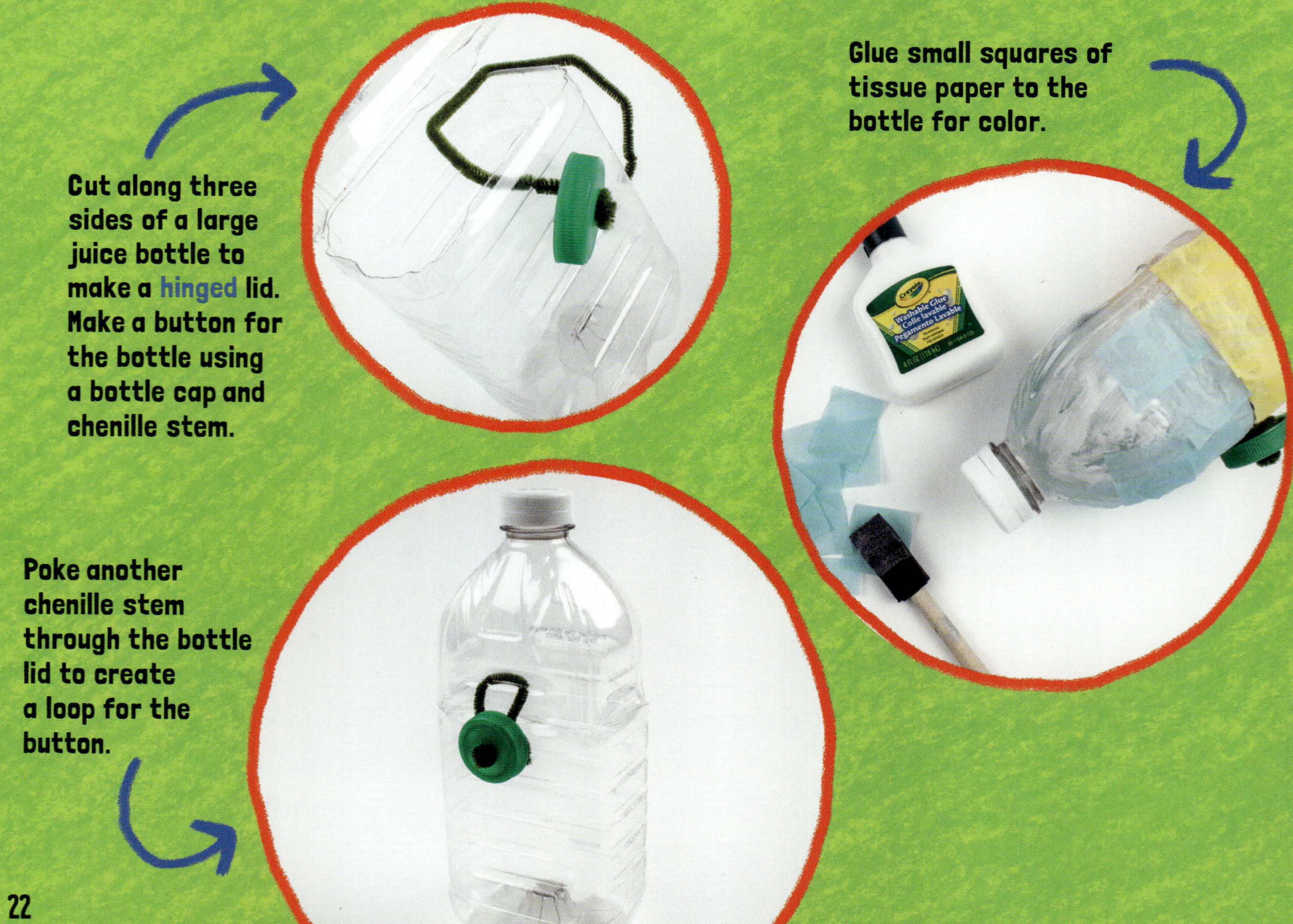

Cut along three sides of a large juice bottle to make a hinged lid. Make a button for the bottle using a bottle cap and chenille stem.

Glue small squares of tissue paper to the bottle for color.

Poke another chenille stem through the bottle lid to create a loop for the button.

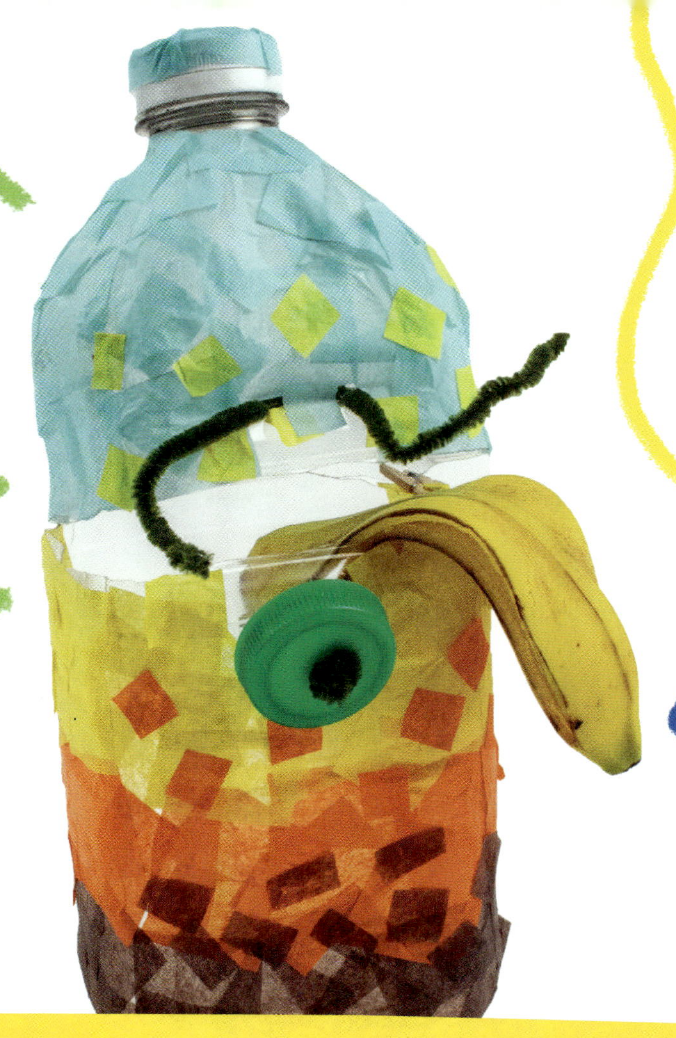

Get Inspired

Think about items you use every day, such as a phone case or pencil holder. Look at these functional items as you come up with your own designs.

Use your bottle as a container to store compost!

Your Turn!

Could you weave chenille stems together to make a coaster?

How could you turn recycled bottles into plant holders?

Could you turn old tissue paper into stuffing for a pillow?

BUILD IT

Engineers use all kinds of materials to build. What do you want to construct? Can you do it using only chenille stems, bottles, and tissue paper?

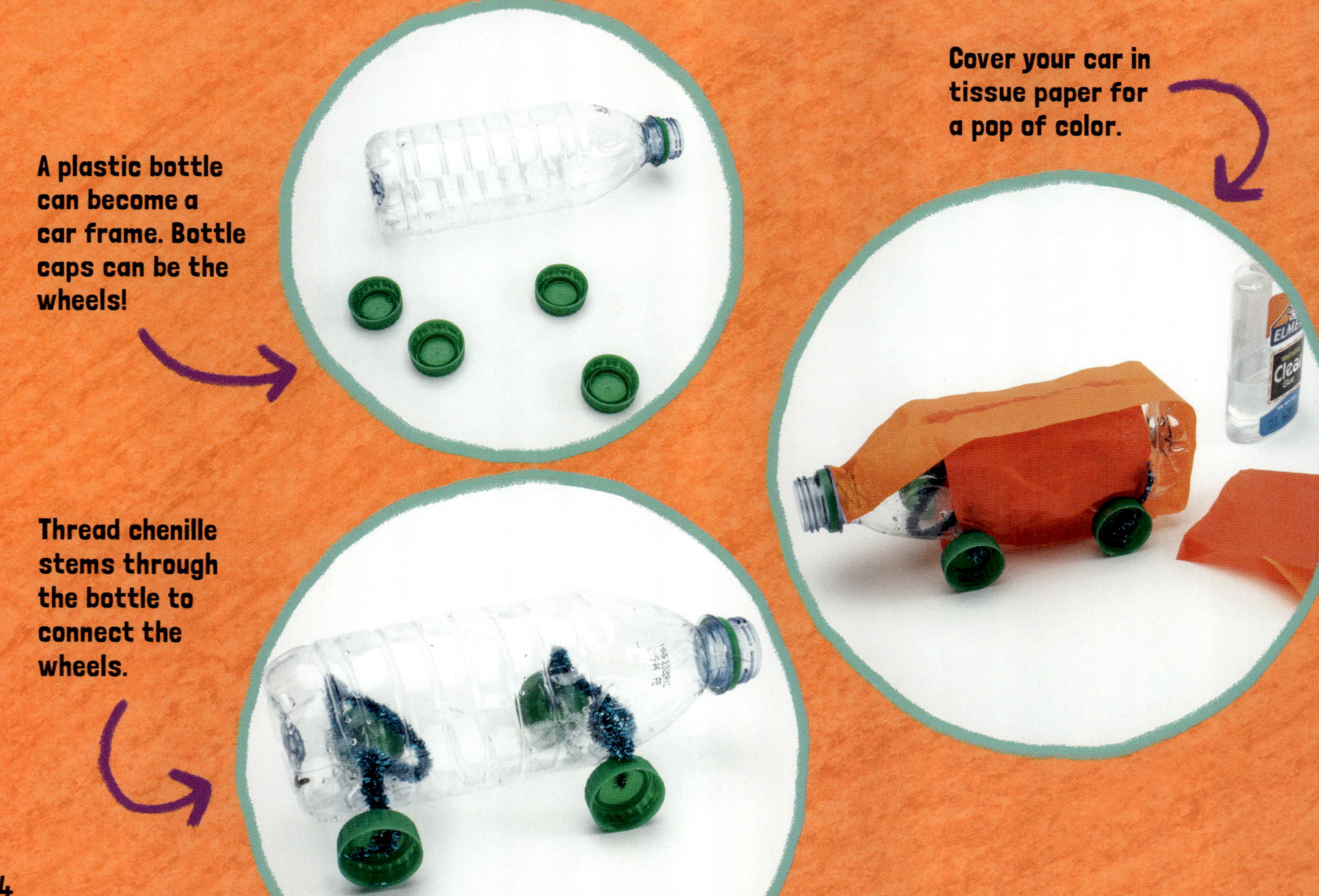

A plastic bottle can become a car frame. Bottle caps can be the wheels!

Cover your car in tissue paper for a pop of color.

Thread chenille stems through the bottle to connect the wheels.

Bend chenille stems into tires, flames, and other details.

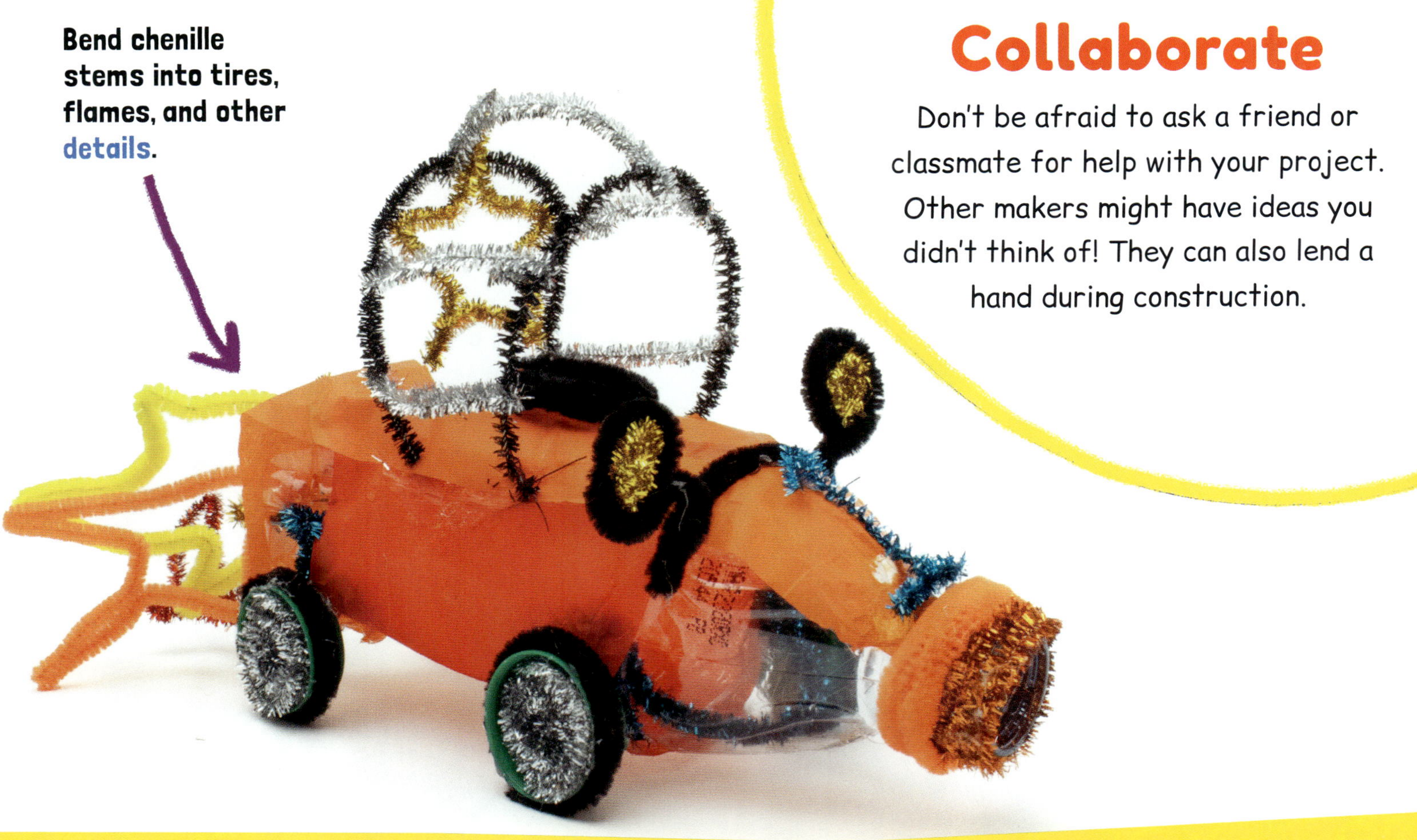

Collaborate

Don't be afraid to ask a friend or classmate for help with your project. Other makers might have ideas you didn't think of! They can also lend a hand during construction.

Your Turn!

How large a tower could you build out of chenille stems?

How would you build a boat out of a soda bottle?

Could you construct a bridge out of braided or twisted tissue paper?

GIFT IT

Is a holiday or birthday coming up? Do you want to surprise a friend or family member just for fun? You can make all kinds of homemade gifts using chenille stems, bottles, and tissue paper.

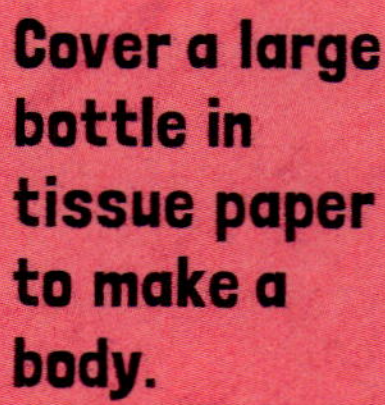

Cover a large bottle in tissue paper to make a body.

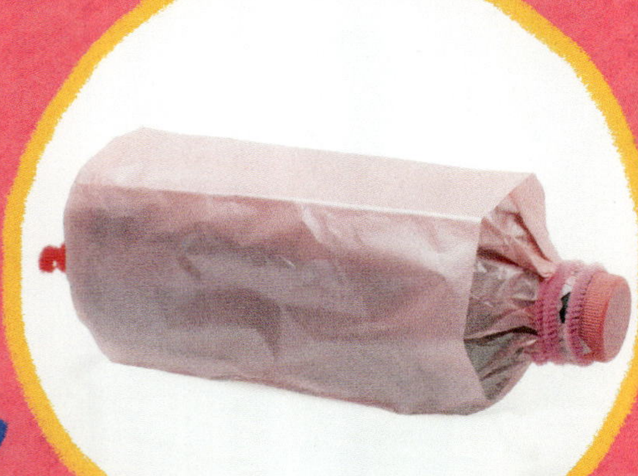

Cut strips out of a plastic bottle. Cover them in tissue paper and chenille stems to make legs.

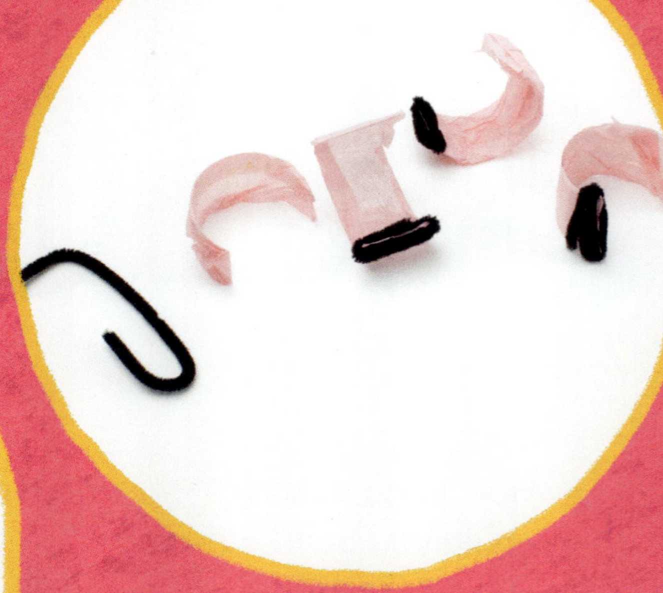

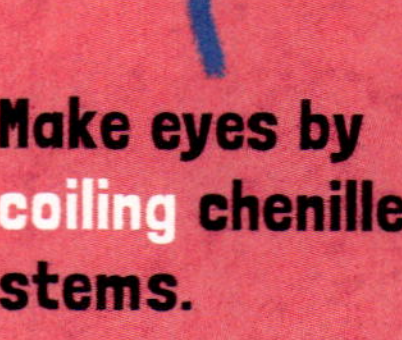

Make eyes by **coiling** chenille stems.

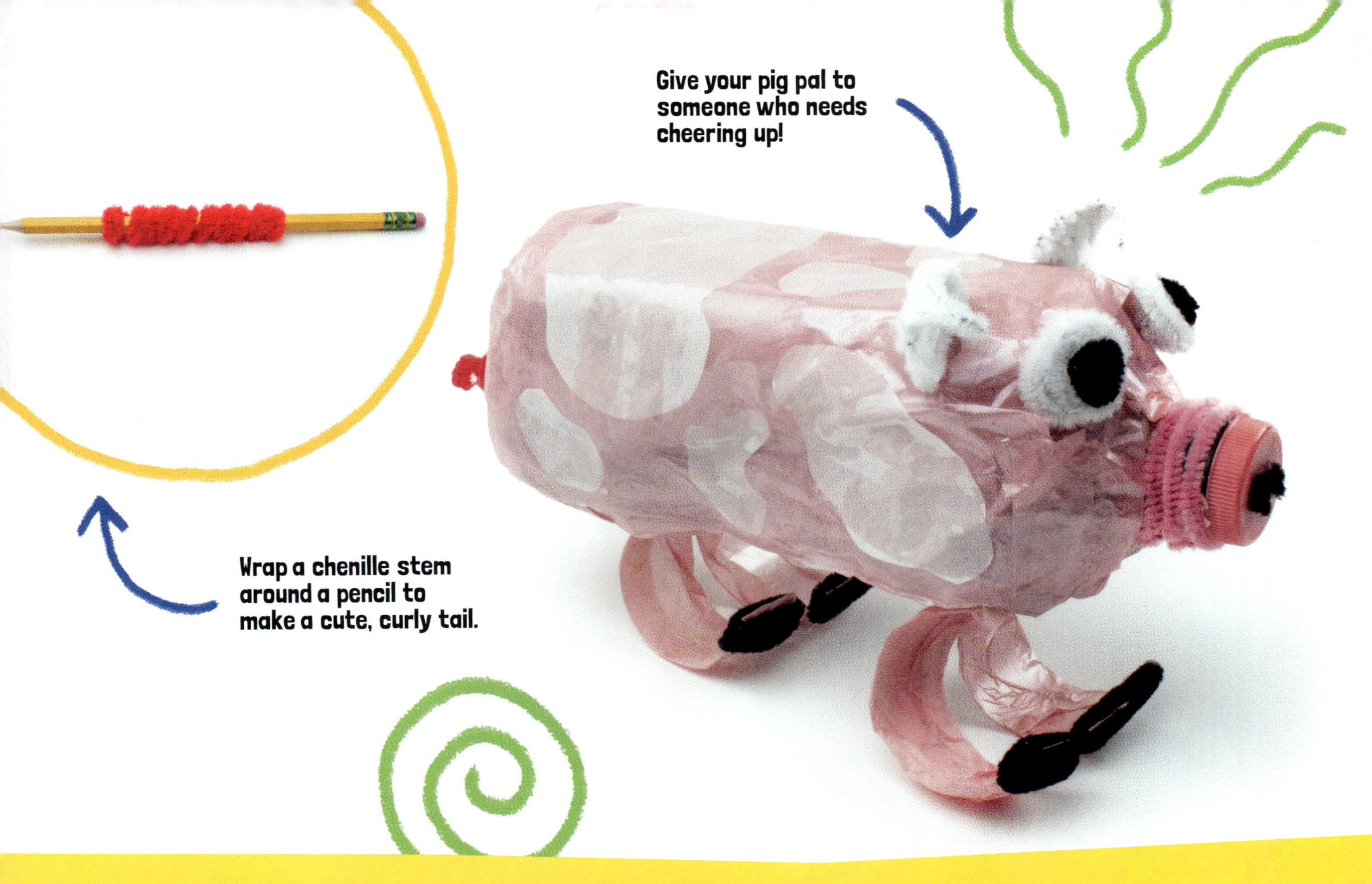

Your Turn!

How might you make a picture frame using chenille stems?

Could you fill a glass bottle with twinkle lights to make a fun desk lamp?

Could you make a vase full of tissue paper flowers?

PLAY WITH IT

Looking for something fun to do? Use chenille stems, bottles, and tissue paper to create your own toys and games!

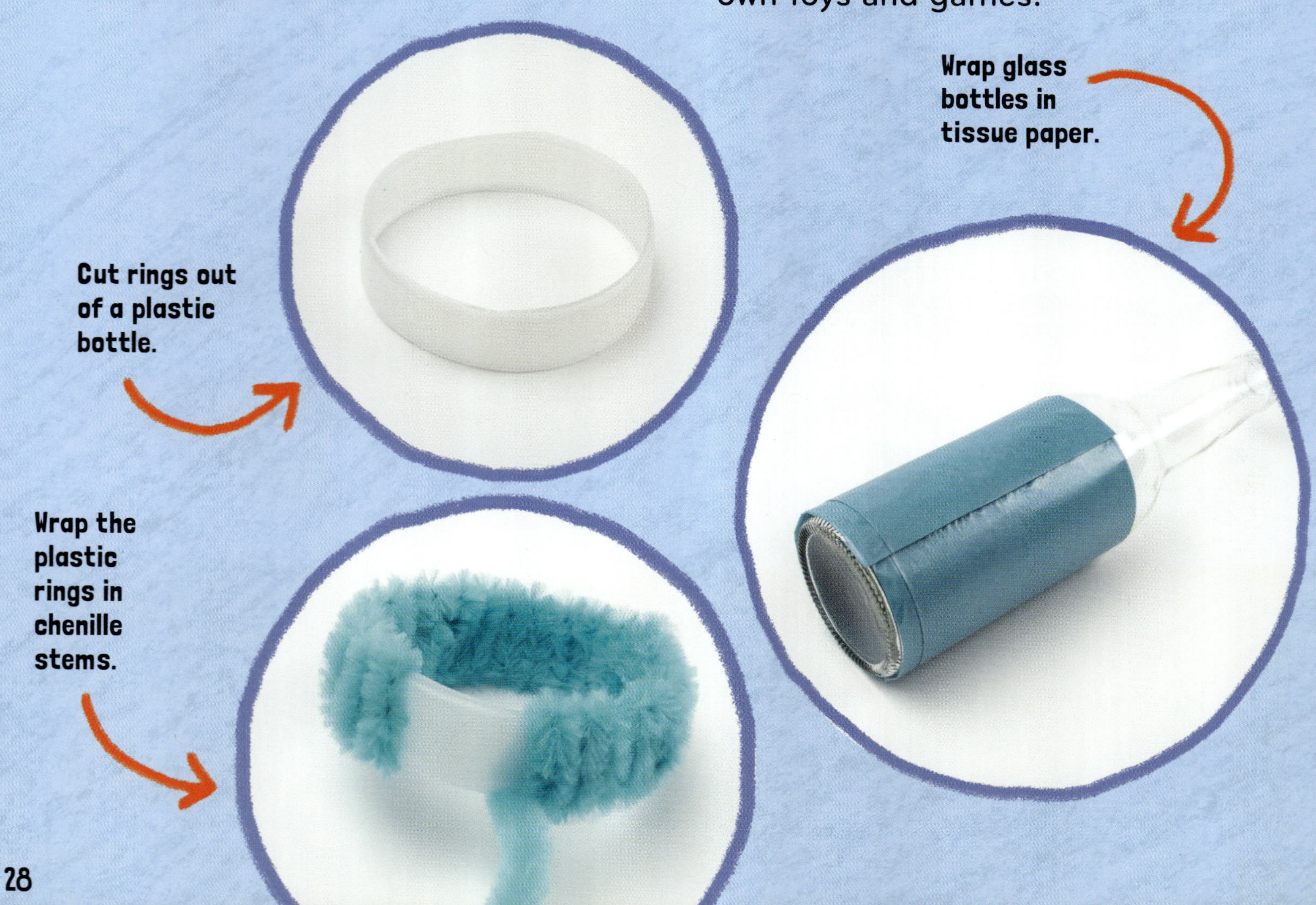

Cut rings out of a plastic bottle.

Wrap glass bottles in tissue paper.

Wrap the plastic rings in chenille stems.

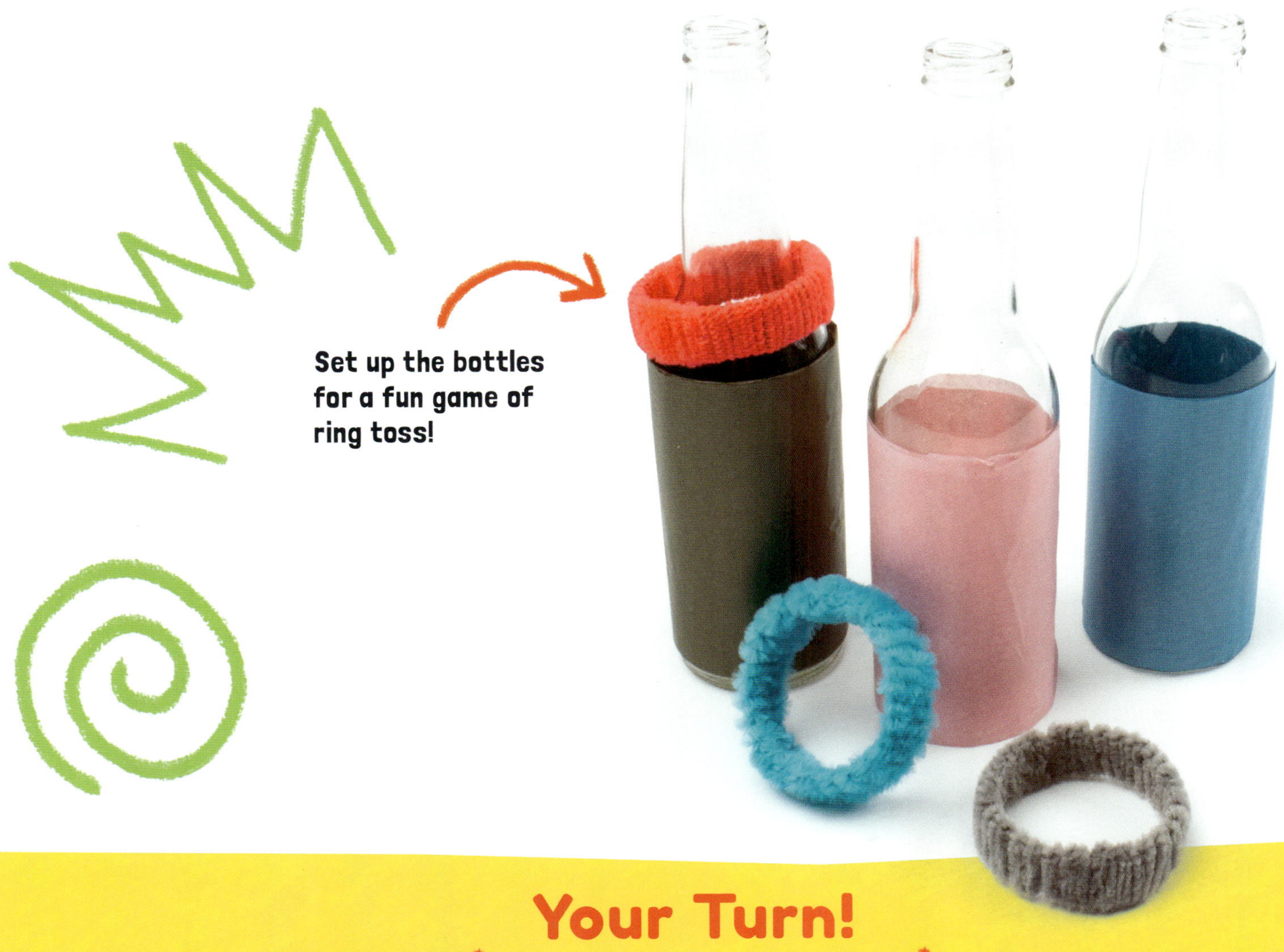

Set up the bottles for a fun game of ring toss!

Your Turn!

How could you make dolls out of chenille stems?

Could you turn bottle caps into game pieces?

Could you make lightweight juggling balls out of tissue paper?

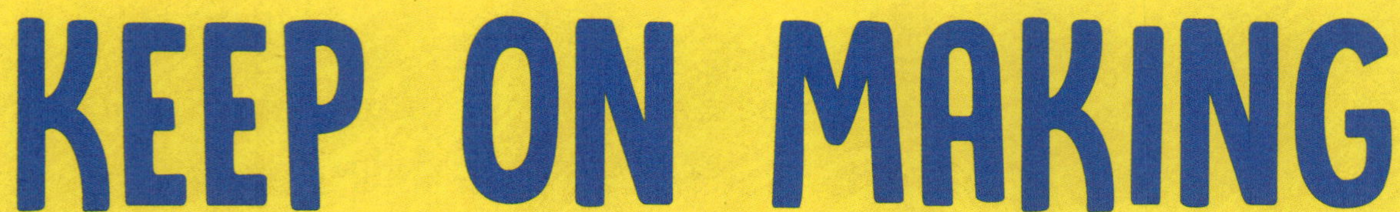

KEEP ON MAKING

Your chenille stem, bottle, and tissue paper projects may look complete, but don't close your makerspace toolbox yet. Think about what would make these projects even better. What would you do differently if you made each one again? What would happen if you used different methods or added another material?

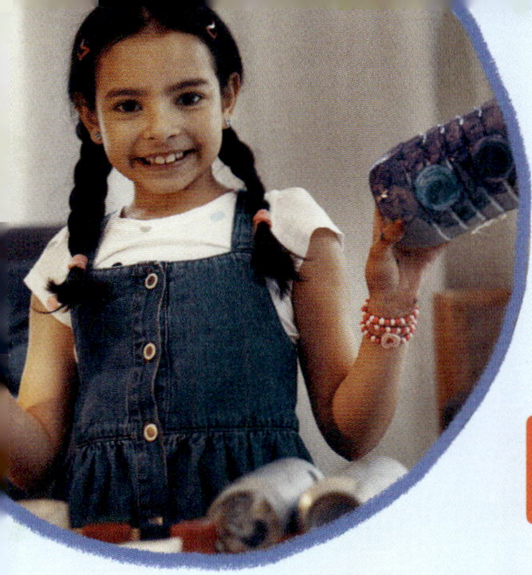

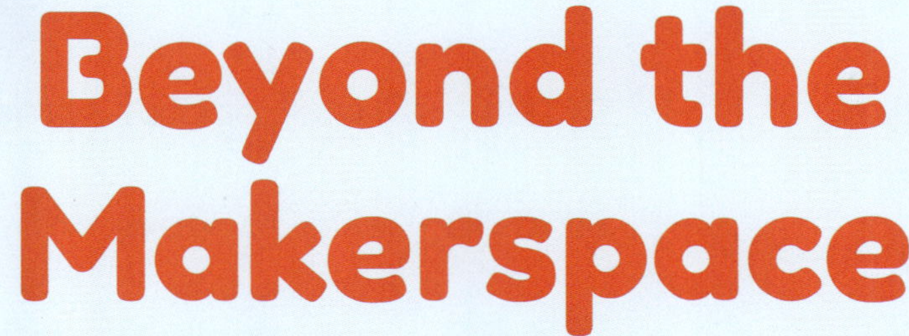

Beyond the Makerspace

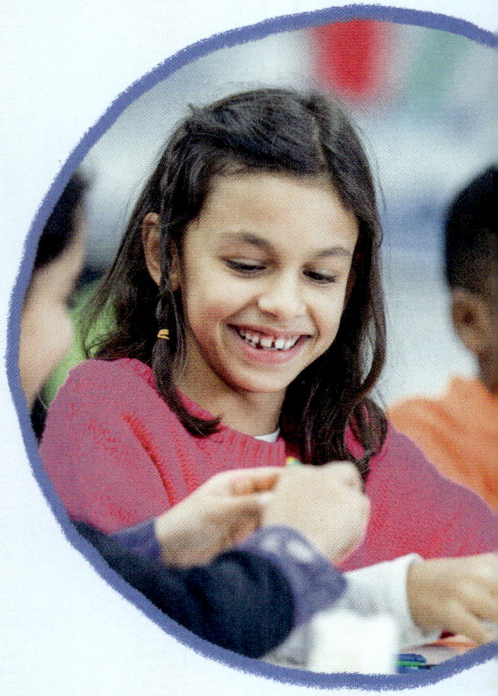

You can use your makerspace toolbox beyond the makerspace! You might use it to accomplish everyday tasks, such as coming up with a science project or a new way to store your toys. But makers use the same toolbox to do big things. One day, these tools could help **design** self-driving cars or new recycling systems. Turn your world into a makerspace! What problems could you solve?

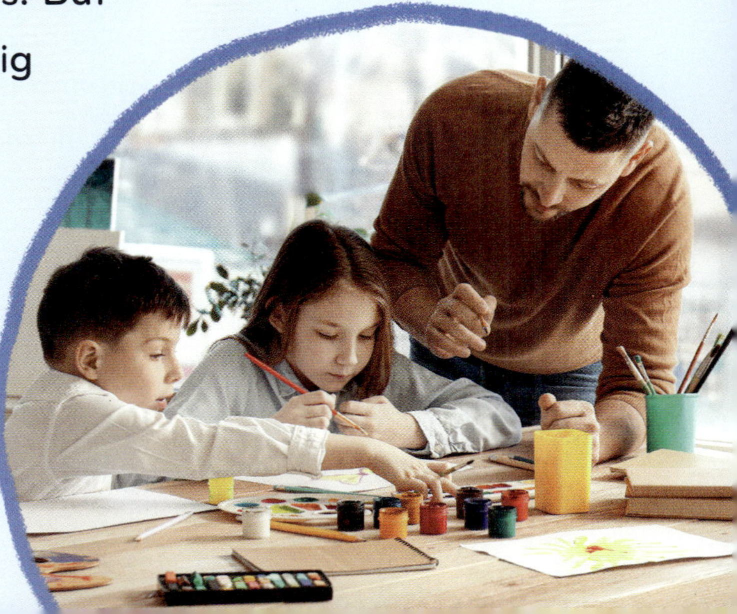

GLOSSARY

accessory – a piece of jewelry or clothing that makes an outfit appear more complete.

coil – to wind or twist into a ring or spiral shape.

collaboration – the act of working with others.

compost – a mixture of natural materials, such as food scraps and lawn clippings, that can turn into fertilizer over time.

container – something that other things can be put into.

design – to plan how something will appear or work. A design is a sketch or outline of something that will be made.

detail – a small part of something.

flexible – easy to move or bend.

folk art – art usually made by unknown artists with no formal training.

garland – a decorative ring or rope made of leaves, flowers, or some other material.

hinged – having a joint that allows two attached parts to move back and forth.

mosaic – a decorative design made up of many small parts.

solution – an answer to, or a way to solve, a problem.

3D – having three dimensions, such as length, width, and height.